my yt mama

ALSO BY MERCEDES ENG

Mercenary English *

Prison Industrial Complex Explodes *

*Published by Talonbooks

my yt mama

poems

Mercedes Eng

Talonbooks

Talonbooks
9259 Shaughnessy Street, Vancouver, British Columbia, Canada V6P 6R4
talonbooks.com

Talonbooks is located on xʷməθkʷəy̓əm, Sḵwx̱wú7mesh, and səlilwətaʔɬ Lands.

First printing: 2020

Typeset in Arno
Printed and bound in Canada on 100% post-consumer recycled paper

Interior and cover design by andrea bennett
On the cover: *whatchamacall3* by Renee Gladman, commissioned for this book, 2019

Talonbooks acknowledges the financial support of the Canada Council for the Arts, the Government of Canada through the Canada Book Fund, and the Province of British Columbia through the British Columbia Arts Council and the Book Publishing Tax Credit.

LIBRARY AND ARCHIVES CANADA CATALOGUING IN PUBLICATION

Title: My yt mama : poems / Mercedes Eng.
Names: Eng, Mercedes, 1972– author.
Identifiers: Canadiana 20190236558 | ISBN 9781772012552 (SOFTCOVER)
Classification: LCC PS8609.N43 M9 2020 | DDC C811/.6—dc23

In the prairies, The Truth is a yt man. The Truth is whatever the yt man says, and whatever truth is said by the yt man is the ruling law of the holy wild wild (prairie) west.

—Lindsay Nixon, *nîtisânak* (2018)

Whereas looking up the word thunderbird I find descriptors such as supernatural which I take to mean not a normal thing. Further I find the thunderbird under a chapter heading Native American Myth and Legends. Whereas I once attended a summer writing program and while there a lecture by a poet on Native American myths. As a student I wanted to stand up at the mic during Q and A to challenge the terms under which one applies the term myth not to mention legend but I did not because the line was long because the speaker was well-known well-respected in other words he was a legend but not a myth. I could not work myself out from under that power nor what was missing and in hesitation / the language / my supernatural chapter ended.

—Layli Long Soldier, *WHEREAS* (2017)

how my yt settler mama met my Chinese immigrant dad

there are different versions of how. I remember my dad telling an exciting story of breaking out of Matsqui Penitentiary in B.C.: scaling the chain-link fence and throwing a jacket over the razor wire at the top so he wouldn't cut himself as he went over it, hiding out through the night in an itchy haystack in a farmer's field adjacent to the pen, before running to Medicine Hat, Alberta to seek sanctuary with his stepdad, the only grandpa I ever knew. grandpa Tai ran an antique store right across the street from the Canadian Pacific Railway station and lived in the basement. mom says dad and other prisoners were getting day passes to go pick strawberries in the many berry fields now occupying unceded Matsqui Territory in the Fraser Valley and there was a rumour that these work permits that granted little bits of freedom would be stopped so he ran away while on one. but both stories begin with dad leaving the prison when he wasn't supposed to and end with dad running to Medicine Hat to hide out at grandpa's. Medicine Hat, where my mom lived her whole life up to that point. they met at a party

race according to my yt mama/1

when I first heard Cher's hit song "half-breed" on the radio
I asked my mom what that was and she said that's you
she was a big fan of 60s/70s Cher who according to my mother
was always glamorous and cool and never
wore the same pair of bell-bottoms twice so
I don't think mom understood that I would
internalize the lyrics of the chorus when trying
to place myself in the prairies of southern Alberta
where the only people who looked like me
were what racist yt people called halfbreeds:
the Métis, and the mixee children of
destatused Indigenous mamas and yt dads

race according to my yt mama/2

the first time I remember being conscious of the violence of race was
when I happened upon my mom watching *Roots*

on the screen a young black woman was being whipped
electric with fear I asked why

because she's black
my mom said, and this uncontextualized response is true but I don't
think she understood what that meant to not-yt me

Mariah according to my yt mama

when I try to talk to my mom about what it was like
to grow up surrounded by yt people in the prairies
in the 80s though it seemed like the 50s
she tells me in a so-there tone
that Mariah is a mixee and that people love her

I tell my mom that Mariah has talked publicly
about feeling some type of way about
being what she calls biracial
which is why on the early album covers
her hair is obscuring her face

there is a long pause then a I didn't know that

I wish her first response wasn't a disavowal of my experience
I wish when I said this to her she didn't disavow my experience again
by telling me that my sibling didn't feel shame about being a mixee
my sibling who in adulthood says
you're more Chinese than me

mood disorder

aiya, the irony of my mental illness
bipolar II matching my biracial blood

me and Mariah
we may not go back like babies with pacifiers
but this is another thing we have in common

dual diagnosis

also called co-occurring disorders, or dual pathology, according to
Wikipedia, *is the condition of suffering from a mental illness and a comor-
bid substance abuse problem*

my addiction was the same as my father's, was
my attempt to ameliorate the symptoms of
my dysfunctional fam my manic depression my bipolarity

is that what he was doing?

in my dad's prison archive there is a report from a drug counsellor
suggesting that mom abused prescription drugs although she has never
admitted a drug problem

they both talked about suiciding

for me being bipolar isn't amazing, I just hate it

when I got my diagnosis I was surprised and immediately was like WHERE are my delusions of grandeur WHY am I not writing award-winning albums and marrying Kim Kardashian and storming across the stage at the VMAs to tell Taylor Swift that the award doesn't belong to her but to Beyoncé even though I'm not into Beyoncé?

the places we come from/0

I was born in a place now known as the City of Medicine Hat

according to Wikipedia:

*The name "Medicine Hat" is the English translation of "Saamis," the
Blackfoot word for the eagle tail feather headdress worn by medicine men.
According to Wikipedia, in 1883, when the Canadian Pacific Railway (CPR)
reached Medicine Hat and crossed the South Saskatchewan River, a townsite
was established. As the west developed, Medicine Hat became instrumental
as a CPR divisional point, as it is the halfway point between Vancouver
and Winnipeg.*

how, do you think, does a direction develop?
how, do you think, does English have such obfuscating power?

In *Saamis: The Medicine Hat*, author Senator F.W. Gershaw explains that there are several *Indian legends* that account for the city's name. Gershaw's book is occasioned by Canada's Centennial which he celebrates by historicizing Medicine Hat, one of the jewels in the crown that is this stolen land now called Canada

according to Gershaw:

there are many theories about the origin of the name and he asks *who used the word "Saamis" first and why*

answering his own question thus:

these are questions that are wrapped in the mysteries of long ago and lost in the limbo of forgotten things

mysteries of long ago, eh?

all of these *legends* have been *passed down* by *pioneers*

in all the legends there are:
warring Cree and Blackfoot tribes
a hat worn by Medicine Men and/or Chiefs

sometimes the hat is a ruse, used to lure one tribe onto the frozen
South Saskatchewan River and then the other tribe jumps out in
surprise attack

sometimes the hat, a *feathery bonnet,* falls off of the head of a Chief
fleeing the attack of the enemy tribe and said enemy tribe takes
possession of the hat

sometimes an *Indian Chief* or a *huge serpent wearing an elaborate head-
dress adorned with plumes* emerges from an opening in the frozen South
Saskatchewan River in front of a brave Blackfoot brave who sacrifices
the maiden of his heart to the *Indian Chief* or *huge serpent in* order to
become the *greatest chief of all the tribes*

sometimes the hat is a *beautiful eagle-feather headdress* made by a *beauti-
ful maiden named Silver Rose* for the Chief who forced her to marry him.
it was in an attempt to appease him

in all the *legends* the place where the medicine hat is positioned/worn/
lost/made is the same: on kisiskāciwani-sīpiy, nehiyawēwin for swift
flowing river

the river is muddy like me they tried to stop us but me & the river we're too fast flowing me & the river we hate this town this town is too small for me & the river the river incited swift movement the river told me to run so my mind did when my body couldn't the river told me to keep moving that if I kept moving I could influence the shape of the landscape

in 1983, as an 11-year-old Girl Guide
the only Guide of colour
the only one who couldn't comfortably use Laurentien pencil crayon
no. 14 for their skin tone
I had to participate in a public celebration of
Medicine Hat's centennial
by memorizing then singing "Hats Off to One Hundred Years," a song
based on a *legend* of how the town got its name

my dad broke out of prison and ran to Medicine Hat to grandpa, whose antique store was right across the street from the CPR station that was built in 1906 and expanded in 1911–1912 to accommodate the city's growing population. my dad stole some horse tranquilizers from a veterinarian and accidentally overdosed on them in the bathroom of the train station so someone called the police and my dad got taken in. he was in real trouble because he had the remainder of his previous bid to serve, plus the time he'd get for breaking out, plus time he'd get for breaking into the veterinary office

for some reason the cops left him uncuffed so he was gonna run. again. but my mom was "in trouble," was nineteen and unmarried and pregnant with me and so he gave up the chance to run for a chance at us being a fam

this story is a legend in my fam

the *legends* of how Medicine Hat got its name don't discuss the agenda and processes of settler colonialism and its ideology of yt supremacy

the *legends* of how Medicine Hat got its name don't speak to us then-girls of colour who internalized yt supremacist ideology so much that we didn't want to be who we were and at times even denied who we were

the *legends* of how Medicine Hat got its name don't explain how ytness invisibilized Indigenous Peoples and people of colour so that I felt like I was the only racialized person even though I wasn't. I mean, my sibling was there. my dad was there when he wasn't in jail though he was mostly in jail. and when I visited him in jail I saw many Indigenous men who were – and continue to be – there because of systemic racism. and there were their families visiting them in jail. and my best friend, my first friend Audra who is Métis though not so much coded that way, and my first love Michelle she was Métis too. so we were there. but I couldn't see us

according to Wikipedia:

Medicine Hat is home to

*the South Alberta Light Horse (SALH), an army reserve unit that dates
back to 1885 when it took part in the North-West Rebellion. Since then it
has gained battle honours in the First and Second World Wars and today
its members serve overseas on United Nations and North Atlantic Treaty
Organization missions. Canadian Forces Base Suffield is located 50 km
west of Medicine Hat and contributes C$120 million annually to the local
economy through its two lodger units: British Army Training Unit Suffield
and Defence Research and Development Canada.*

is home to war research and readiness

is home to   fire-watered Thatcherite soldiers
            dancing cold war circuits of desire
            in a nuclear date rape bomb shelter
            my lover's destatused mama
            blood sampling your
            genetically modified diseases

is home to some of the largest gas fields on Turtle Island

is home to the world's tallest *teepee*

the love songs I couldn't listen to during a research trip back "home" to finish this book on the land on which I first fell in love, for fear that I would have a breakdown

"love will tear us apart" / Joy Division
"just like heaven" / the Cure
"bizarre love triangle" / New Order
any Velvet Underground
any Pixies
any Smiths
any Jesus and Mary Chain

our journeys through cities as they existed for us when we were young and in love: sue and jane write a story together/1

on the muddy banks of the South Saskatchewan River we giggled together, squatted down watching the methane bubbles break the surface of our river. in our shitty city not looking yt meant being 11 or 12 and getting called "china boy" only to develop boobs and suddenly it becomes "unique, almond-shaped eyes" with "fuck you" racing through my brain. I ran away and ran away and ran away to meet my love, and we were given shelter by a yt boy Dustin who went out to hook on the gay boys' stroll to come "home" with a loaf of yt bread for us all to eat. there was another yt queer who sheltered us, Lise, a femme whose wardrobe staple was a hooded red-velvet cape that reached the floor though she was a bit more wolf than girl in the woods

if only we had known about Chrystos and her poem "White Girl Don't": sue and jane write a story together/2

why was everything so wrong? busted little halfbreeds dragged off the Greyhound. gotcha little lovers escaped from a group home. milk box Van city kids panning for cinnamon buns

please don't take me away from her: sue and jane write a story together/3

we are never not meeting at a tumultuous time but we carry one another wherever and whenever we go because of the biological process of wound repair in the skin that marks us

yt prairie mamas and five generations of Ellens

my yt great-grandmother Ellen
migrated from Sweden to the "new world" at 17

my yt grandma's middle name is Eleonora

my yt mama's middle name is Ellen

me, her mixee daughter's middle name is Ellen

her mixee granddaughter's middle name is Ellen

I wonder if the latest Ellen will have kids and if

she has a girl will she choose to carry on the tradition

Chinese and yt grandmas

when I was a kid my mom referred to my maternal grandma as
"grandma"
but called my paternal grandma
"Chinese grandma"
she still does it though I've told her how problematic it is
and how would it be if I called her mom
"yt grandma"
she scoffs

P.S.

I think my mom is getting nervous about this book because I told her
about this poem and the very next time she referred to my father's mother
she simply said "grandma"

yt supremacist beauty standard/1

when she was 10
my beautiful young cousin asked me
don't you wish you had blue eyes
like Taylor Swift like celebrities

it broke my heart
that a generation later
the desire for blue eyes
still reigns supreme

yt supremacist beauty standard/2

my mom has skin the colour
of the eggs I grew up eating in Alberta

when I visited my grandma in Vancouver
I resisted eating her brown eggs

I don't even remember the last time I bought yt eggs

I got the yt supremacy blues

May 2015

Dear Kendrick,

are you really a fan of Taylor Swift? do you really love that song with that hook that makes me want to stab myself in the temple? really, a 20-year-old yt girl who appropriates black culture, singing an empty song composed of phrases stolen from your people?

well, maybe I'm a 42-year-old half Chinese half yt woman who appropriates black culture through speech too. I don't know about Taylor Swift's father, but I know that my father spent a lot of time in prison like a lot of black American men and my "talking black" is me using my father's non-standard-English-as-a-second language he learned at the school of hard knocks.

maybe I shouldn't judge this yt girl. maybe I'm just a hater, and you know, haters *gonna hate hate hate*

but my young cousin says she wants to have blue eyes because Taylor Swift has blue eyes

as a half Chinese half yt woman who is often misread as an Indigenous person – people who in both your nation and "mine" have experienced genocide at the hands of yt people – I hated being a mixee kid and couldn't wait to grow up so I could buy blue-coloured contacts and dye my hair blonde and try to pass as a Hitler youth. it took me years to get over this idea of beauty as ytness.

so when a generation later my lil' cuz expresses a wish for blue eyes because Taylor Swift has blue eyes, it makes me want to
burn down a city

but I guess you're just a player who's *gonna play play play*

so I guess I'll just try to *shake it off, shake it off, shake it off*

yours sincerely,
Mercedes Eng

May 2019

P.S.

I couldn't even listen to *To Pimp a Butterfly* cuz I was so angry at you. but I missed you and damn, is *DAMN* fire

Each night, without fail, she prayed for blue eyes. Fervently, for a year she had prayed. Although somewhat discouraged, she was not without hope. To have something as wonderful as that happen would take a long, long time.

—Toni Morrison, *The Bluest Eye* (1970)

my beauty standard

on the prairies of southern Alberta
I was surrounded
by yt women who looked nothing like me

where their necks were short mine was long
where their asses were flat mine was juicy
where their hair was thin mine was full
where they were wide I was slender as
a stroke of calligraphy on an oracle bone

rice

my father's mother was the first girl in her fam with unbound feet, certainly she had an unbound mind so she knew what it was to have a fast-flowing river inside her too but her river was Zhū Jiāng and when it told her to run she did. the same when my grandpa Tai died and she got his money, running to Reno or Vegas with her girlfriends to gamble or staying home to listen to Cantonese opera records and play mah-jong for money and drink Johnnie Walker Black

potatoes

my yt grandma once asked me "who do you think you are, the Queen of Sheba?" why yes yt grandma I do believe I'm a hawt biblical queen of colour wreaking havoc and generally causing a ruckus because unlike you I dreamed beyond this town this river valley this province this nation state this gender

but it's not all her fault she was constantly reminding me not to get too big for my britches cause she was born and raised in a time when women didn't wear pants, like, she didn't wear pants until her 70s and I don't remember her in a dress after my mom got her to try pants. my yt grandma was someone you'd want around when the apocalypse that yt people keep making movies about gets here, although the apocalypse is already here. you'd want her around because for decades she grew all the food she ate except sugar, coffee, and flour. planted seeds, tended plants, ate of the harvest. since she was in single digits, helping her fam in the fields, bragged by her father to be "strong as an ox." I haven't contributed to the growing of food that I eat since I was a child and when I did it was with my yt grandma

a song for Audra's Métis mother

I dedicated my first book
not to my mother but to
Terrylynn Rivard McDonald
the mother of my childhood best friend, Audra

Terry is the only one I remember
believing in my dream of being a writer
asking me about my dream of being a writer
making me believe that shit was possible

she never judged me or my crazy fam
when other mothers yt mothers
wouldn't allow their children to play with me
because my dad was a drug addict a convict
because he wasn't yt

a song for Audra's Métis grandmother

sovereign nation of her body named
after the grandmother of Europe
given to Jesus to the convent at 8
the way to godliness is cleanliness of
mother superior's menses cloths

so when the adopted son of the Rivards
rolled up and said I'm a cowboy, baby
she said let's fucking ride
and they did

a song for my yt mama

I wish I could write a song for my mom
like Tupac did for his dear mama

me and Tupac, cradled in amniotic fluid
the first time we entered the walls of a prison

Tupac's mama was a Black Panther who resisted the system
my mom is the system

the crazy things my mother told me when I was a kid

that life isn't fair

that when I was a baby I bit her so to teach me not to bite she bit my baby limb hard enough to leave a black-and-blue ring "for weeks" and I "never bit her again"

that Hitler wouldn't have let me live just because I was half yt. rather, because I was yt and Chinese mixed together, I was the worst as far as he was concerned

I remember my mom coming home with a big book of black-and-yt World War II photographs, one of the books the public library was giving away. there was a picture of some broad steps on which a whole bunch of people's bodies and parts were scattered and there was this disconnected little baby leg with its sock and shoe still on. I was 5, 6 maybe. the pictures of Hitler were scary. he looked really mad and mean like a cop. I remember asking my mom about the war and her telling me about Nazis and how only blond-haired blue-eyed people were desired and how he killed all these Jewish people because they weren't and I remember asking about me, if he would gas chamber me because I was, after all, part German too

she, unlike so many other prejudiced people in our shitty town, didn't see my dad as less than because he wasn't yt, because he was a convict, a junkie, but I don't think she understood the impact of what she said, that in a not-so-far-away country and in a not-so-far-away time I might have been exterminated

that life isn't fair

that my parents' friend Kelly was a stripper (not such a big deal) and also a hooker (a bit bigger of a deal but she was glamorous and she was really nice and I really liked her) and that the prize for some amateur boxing match going on in town was her or a night with her anyway

that if my father got her sent to prison she would suicide by drowning herself in the cell sink

that Richard Pryor had grown a beard because he was freebasing too much and needed it to hide his skinny face so people wouldn't know

that she didn't have to have me

my mom was an orphan, was adopted, so that's the place she's coming from when she said she didn't have to have me but when I was 15 I didn't understand that what she meant was

I kept you when my own mother gave me away

my grandma and grandpa picked her up from a hospital in Calgary and brought her back home to their farm near Medicine Hat, a homesteading plot on Treaty 7 Territory

apparently her birth mother was also from Medicine Hat but didn't deliver there. I surmise that her birth mother was a young woman "in trouble" and she did what a young woman did if she lived in a small town and she got "in trouble": she went to a big city to get rid of her trouble so that getting rid of her trouble was more anonymous

my mom knows her birth name, first middle last, so someone named her if not claimed her and then the only mom she ever knew renamed her and we began working on five generations of Ellens

that life isn't fair

that if she got into an accident because of her speeding she'd rather not wear a seatbelt so as to incur a fatal injury and just die right away instead of wearing one and possibly ending up "in a wheelchair or something"

"that's you" when we heard Diana Ross and the Supremes' hit song "love child" on the radio and I asked what a love child was

that my dad had met Jimi Hendrix and Ray Charles and had scored heroin for one of them (she can't remember which one now, but my dad told me he met Hendrix at the Smilin' Buddha and I know Hendrix did play a show there)

that life isn't fair

that she couldn't go to the police about my dad beating her because he would kill her (which I guess is why I spent my 11th summer at the women's shelter, because she finally did, and he didn't)

that instead of taking his youngest and favourite sister's sick and elderly dog to the vet to be put down, my dad gave the dog, named Trudeau after the 1969 Yt Paper prime minister, a shot of heroin

that she wouldn't let my dad teach me Chinese because she was worried about what he might say that she wouldn't be able to understand

that my first Halloween costume was a onesie she drew convict stripes on, my dad's prison number on my baby breast

that life isn't fair

that she didn't breastfeed me because you couldn't do that in the prison visiting rooms and she didn't want to have to run out to the bathroom every time I needed milk

in Toni Morrison's novel *Beloved,* to Sethe the protagonist, the biggest crime isn't the rapes or beatings she experiences, the biggest crime against her is that they stole her milk

that life isn't fair

in her memoir *Heart Berries* Terese Marie Mailhot recalls dreaming the smell of her milk on her absent baby's breath

that life isn't fair

what black and Indigenous women and their children have experienced is nothing like my mom not breastfeeding me. when I read what Morrison and Mailhot write about mother's milk it makes me cry like a baby needing milk

that life isn't fair

in Eden Robinson's novel *Son of a Trickster* the protagonist Jared's mom
says "life is hard, you have to be harder" which made me think of my
mom and her "life isn't fair." both mine and Jared's moms are often
unable to be present parents, and Eden says Jared's mom is coming
from a place of trauma. my mom's coming from a place of trauma too

the places we come from/1

a branch of kisiskāciwani-sīpiy (the Saskatchewan River) flows through Treaty 7 Territory, the last of the Numbered Treaties to be negotiated, signed in 1877. Treaty 7 includes the cities of Medicine Hat, Calgary, Lethbridge, Red Deer, and several small towns and villages

kisiskāciwani-sīpiy flows through the centre of Medicine Hat, which was established as a townsite once the CPR built a bridge across the river

part of the Cypress Hills is in Treaty 7 Territory and traverses the border between the provinces of Alberta and Saskatchewan into Treaty 4 Territory

traverses borders like me
traverses borders like my yt mama did
when she loved my not-yt dad
and didn't give a fuck
what anyone in our shitty prairie town thought
about their love
that produced me

according to Gershaw, that is, according to the yt man's Truth, the North-West Mounted Police (NWMP) was formed in response to the Cypress Hills Massacre. Calls for a police force to protect yt settlers in what was then called the North-West Territories, and to protect the Canadian border from American whiskey traders because these *heartless traders robbed and debauched* the Indigenous Peoples, had already been sent to the nation state's capitol. then the massacre occurred: American traders *seeking revenge* for allegedly stolen horses *ambushed a peaceful camp of* Indigenous Peoples, slaughtering thirty of them. so a decision was made and a call was made and some 300 *brave boys began an adventure west* and became the NWMP

sun dances, *with all their savage cruelty,* were held in the Cypress Hills until outlawed by the yt man

the legend of Ky-yo-kosi/Bear Child

Jerry Potts was a mixed-race man who worked for the North-West
Mounted Police for 22 years as guide and interpreter, and is credited
with negotiating the neutrality of the Blackfoot Confederacy during the
North West *Rebellion*

according to Wikipedia:

As a person of mixed blood, he had to prove to both Métis and yts that
he could cope in their respective cultures, and was well served by his quick
wits, reckless bravery, skills with the knife, and lethal accuracy with both a
revolver and a rifle.

this Wikipedia entry creates a legend of a mixed-race Indigenous person
who colluded with, not resisted, settlers

most of this Wikipedia entry is cut and pasted from the University of
Toronto / Université Laval's online *Dictionary of Canadian Biography* so
the legend of Potts is official Canadian history

in Gershaw's legend of Medicine Hat, the arrival of the railway is pivotal to the formation of the township as is NWMP. he begins his legend of the NWMP by stating that *the great work of the police was to stamp out the whiskey smuggling, to protect the few yt settlers, and to make a law-abiding race out of the wandering bands* of Indigenous Peoples. in the middle of his NWMP legend which is in the middle of his Medicine Hat legend is his legend of Potts which is mainly about how Potts's yt father was killed by an Indigenous person who Potts arduously searches for and when found he and the killer fight *tooth and nail* with *tomahawks and knifes* with Potts delivering *the fatal blow.* his legend of the NWMP concludes by stating that they *brought law and order into a wild and lawless country*

the legend of the craft brewery
of Medicine Hat

so in 2016 Bro #1, Bro #2, and Bro #3 opened a craft brewery named
after an Indigenous vehicle of conveyance that the Niitsítapi Peoples
call "imatáá manistsí" which *were used by Great Plains aboriginal bands
to haul their stuff. It usually consisted of two long poles with some sort of
framework, lashed to the sides of your dog, and the frame carried your
tipi and food*

your dog? your tipi and food? are these cowbros trying to play *Indian*?

*Early fur trappers trekking through the Canadian West, and even the
RCMP, copied it. As such, travois are an iconic part of Medicine Hat's
early history and are intrinsically connected to this part of the world, they
are uniquely prairie ... like us ... and they represent travel and movement
through the great outdoors* love for which brought the bros together

so Bro #1 met Bro #2 who had enough money to acquire a building
downtown even though he didn't even know what he was gonna do
with it, although not the original building that was located on Montreal
Street back in the founding days of Medicine Hat which is *lost to time*
but the building now in that location which was built in 1939

45

so they started talking about turning the building into a brewery and realized they'd need more money so that's where Bro #3 who Bro #1 knew from the Cypress Hills biking trails comes into the legend: Bro #3 was *a casualty of the latest oil-patch recession and was looking for something to fuel his dreams rather than just his pocketbook*

I'm not a craft brewery person myself as I see them as agents of gentrification and I'm anti-gentrification or more accurately I'm anti-gentrification-as-an-ongoing-instantiation-of-colonialism-and-yt-supremacy as I'm assuming that most craft breweries are owned by yt guys who wanna create these legends about the genesis of their businesses like they're some kind of frontiersmen boldly going where no one's ever gone before

... so come on down, see what we've done with the place, try the beer ... and don't forget to bring your dog and travois to haul your growler home

why u staring?

while in Medicine Hat to finish this book I go into a bargain store and am followed then questioned about where the shirt is that I tried on even though the clerk can see I'm holding the shirt that I tried on. Michelle says maybe they thought I was a meth tourist – Medicine Hat now has another nickname besides the Hat which is Meth Hat and Lethbridge is Methbridge. Audra says maybe it was my weight and my hair. there I'm thin enough to be mistaken for a meth addict and my hair is obviously bottle blonde. or I look like I'm not from there so whether racism or xenophobia or prejudice against people with health issues, who knows? but people are also friendly. my plan is to walk to the train station, to the City Café and my grandfather's antique store which are on the same block across from the station. I used to go to the café with my fam all the time; my favourite waitress was named Gypsy or we called her Gypsy anyway, who had long black hair and tawny skin and LOVE tattooed across her knuckles. the café has been renamed and renovated and turned into a vegan restaurant that more than one person had recommended to me. maybe I look like a vegan? but these yt people, they get served before me even though I came in before them and am bodily communicating that I'm ready to order. the waitress who is not at all cool like Gypsy doesn't check on me or refill my water glass though it's empty

Michelle says she remembers this happening to her and her mother often. I don't remember this with my mother but then my mama is yt

how my father saw my yt mama

unlike my dad's mostly realist copper engravings
don't ask's surrealist imagery perplexed me as a kid

an emaciated male figure holding a set of scales
rides a skinny horse across a vast desert
lines of longitude radiating out to provide perspective
an oversized broken syringe
an hourglass in the foreground
the vanishing point a ballerina, my yt mama, pirouetting
at the base of a castle-topped mountain
my yt mama the vanishing point
my yt mama the muse

how I saw my yt mama

while in group therapy for drug recovery we did a lot of art
and one exercise was to create an image of our moms

a feminized figure composed of puzzle pieces outlined in red
a big question mark at the centre of her head

how my yt mama saw my father

I think my mom saw my dad like a lot of women saw my dad

well proportioned and fit as fuck
long thick straight black hair
sharp cheekbones wide smile
easy laugh charm for miles
tattoos that said I got a story you wanna hear
a visible lack of underpants that said I'm ready

I learned three things watching my mother:
1. No one can fuck their way to tolerance.
2. No one can marry into tolerance.
3. No one can carry for nine months and give birth to tolerance.

—Alicia Elliott, *A Mind Spread Out on the Ground* (2019)

how I saw my father

he stood out. because everyone knows everything in a small town, every-one knew my dad as a druggie and a wife beater who was regularly in and out of prison, and I was ashamed of him. to me his badness was marked physically through clothing and race. he dressed very differently than the other adults in our town, especially in the summer: super-short jean cut-offs with no underwear beneath, no shirt either, revealing his many prison tattoos, mirrored aviator sunglasses, big jade ring set in solid gold with whorls like dragon smoke. as a kid I hated my dad because he hurt my mom and terrified me and because he was Chinese, I hated it in me. I didn't wanna be like him. the few other Chinese people in town weren't like him, but that fell outside my vision; that his fam was actually better educated, higher on the economic ladder, didn't register. for me this wife-beating, jail-going, drug-using difference was inextricably linked to race. I wanted that Chineseness out. and I didn't just want to be yt, I wanted to be the right kind of yt. I wanted blue eyes and blonde hair, and when I got older and had money, I was gonna dye my hair and get blue-coloured contacts. I didn't then know about skin-ytning creams. my non-ytness not only meant that I could never be popular at school, it's also what marked me out to be sexually abused. like when a relative on my mother's side sexually abused me in my grandma's basement while playing hide and seek, I knew it could happen to me because of what I was: not-yt, or maybe what I wasn't: yt. when a relative on my father's side sexually abused me, it could happen to me because I was less than, because I wasn't quite Chinese and my dad was a bad Chinese person unlike the child molester. as an adult I learned that the yt relative had done the same thing to a yt cousin. so I was wrong, it didn't happen because of my otherness, because of not being yt enough on the one side and not being Chinese enough on the other, it happened because some people are super fucked up and think they can hurt children

what we are /what they see

my friend Michelle who is Métis
was called a chink as a child

I'm half Chinese half yt
but am typically pheneticized as Indigenous

Sheryl, Michelle's sister, is Métis
but could pass as half Japanese half yt

my friend Echo is Chinese
but is sometimes pheneticized as half Japanese half yt

you're a yt lady/1

my best friend Echo has called me a yt lady
more than once
and it feels like an accusation
though I think what she's saying
is I'm uptight or bougie

Echo's mama goes on a trip to Korea
returns with many K-beauty products
including the bestselling Laneige BB Cushion

she bought Echo the darkest shade but it was still too light
for her skin so Echo gave it to me but it was too light
for my skin so I gave it to my best friend Emily who has
blond hair and blue eyes and it was perfect for her skin

you're a yt lady/2

after months of trying to get my partner
who's been spoiled by his mama and titas
to reciprocate and do his share of the cooking
I suggest making up a schedule for taking turns
and he says that's a yt people thing
and it feels like an accusation

**in response to my question of if there had
ever been a desire for ytness: I never wanted
to be yt/1**

"I always knew I was cute."

—Queen Echo

**in response to my question of if there had
ever been a desire for ytness: I never wanted
to be yt/2**

"No."

—my partner

the places we come from/2

Drumheller is located in the Red Deer River Valley. wāwaskesiw-sīpiy (the Red Deer River) meets with both the northern and southern arms of the Saskatchewan River to empty into Lake Winnipeg in Manitoba connecting the prairie provinces through moving water

Drumheller Institution was built in 1967
to celebrate Canada's centennial, do you think?

as a kid I have been to Drumheller countless times to visit my dad in the pen but have never been to the Royal Tyrrell Museum and even now at the mention of visiting the museum
my inner child swims rapidly to the surface
crying seething resentful

seeing my dad in this place this place that was the only place where I saw large groups of people of colour made ever-more fervent the desire to look like my blue-eyed fair-skinned mother

rideshare

my mom used to give rides to women whose men were inside men who
when they found out that mom was driving from Medicine Hat to one
of the prisons around Southern Alberta asked my dad if my mom could
help them out

one girl when we went to McDonald's for lunch only bought a large
orange pop but no food for her and her 2-year-old son so my mom
bought them lunch

my mom was giving rides since before I can remember

if you understood how hard the prison industrial complex works to isolate
prisoners from their blood and chosen fams you would understand how
important this labour of my mother's was

strip search

one time at Drumheller pen the male guards wanted to strip search the women and the children before a visit. which I'm pretty fucking sure is illegal but the yt man says what is illegal and what isn't. I don't remember any male visitors though there could have been. my mom refused to let these yt men touch her or her children and it helped the other mothers to refuse too

she tore a strip off him

maybe she could refuse the guards because when she was a child
a yt man hurt her
so when the yt man said I am going to invade
the bodies of you and your children she said
never again, motherfucker

west: elemental/1

water mother   fire daughter

east: elemental/2

water dragon mother   water rat daughter

this body

this body is mix & match
this body is muddy
this body is miscegenated
this body is misgauged
this body is miscoded
this body is cherry blossom cheeks and
                    "bbq pork-scented sorrow," clotted cream
                    and schnitzel
this body doesn't belong
this body doesn't belong to anyone
this body is heavy with stories
this body is lonely
this body is a freshet
this body is an estuary
this body is knowledge
this body sets fires
this body is alleged
this body is the dust of life
this body is mad
this body is bipolar
this body is biracial
this body is bifurcated
this body is in parts
this body is kintsugi

this body is social act
this body is a longitudinal study on the effects of
          colonialism and racism and exoticization
this body is sovereign though Fred Moten teaches
          that sovereignty was never intended this body
          & Billy-Ray Belcourt teaches this body that some bodies
          are unbodied & Sarah Hunt teaches sovereignty and
          bodies matter
this body is a blood memory
this body is irreducible
this body holds ancestors
this body is dissent
this body is deficit
this body is deficient
this body is defaced
this body is desired
this body is delinquent
this body is a reliquary
this body is a full cellar
this body is a luxury problem
this body is discount Cartier
this body is nouveau riche
this body is niche
this body is askew
this body ascends
this body descends
this body is subterranean
this body is place
this body is a border crossing

this body is taking space
this body is itinerant
could this body be medicine?
this body is indexical
this body is ephemeral
this body is star-seeded
this body is transgressive
this body is vernacular melanin
this body is sick and tired
this body is rhizomatic
this body is wanted
this body is sustainable
this body is pressure
this body is contact zone
this body is cusp
this body is dawn
this body is dusk
this body is door
this body is window
this body is midnight
this body is noon
this body is economically sound
this body is depreciating
this body is planted through with Oregon grape
this body is a seed bomb
this body drops seed bombs
            all over this thing called the city
this body does it wrong
this body is a university

this body is little sister
this body is big sister
this body holds all her sisters
this body is a beginning
this body is a coyote route
this body is a story
this body is paradoxical
this body is a small detail
this body is not a single event
this body is in arrears
this body is never good enough for some
this body is enough for many
this body is extra and Mama Ru says
                        shantay, you stay
this body is a love letter
this body is aflame
this body is a cycle
this body is a ship
this body is clear pure sound
this body is in process
this body is woo woo
this body is thunderstorms
this body is a suitcase
this body is a palimpsest
this body is an unreliable narrator
this body is question
this body is answer
this body is conundrum
this body has a lot to say

this body is transcendent
this body is perfect
this body doesn't need to be fixed
this body is a murder of crows
this body is a pack of stray dogs
this body is
this body is
this body is
this body is incongruent
this body is grease stained
this body is every Mariah dance track
                that made you wanna move your body
this body is emotions
this body's gonna make it happen
this body is fantasy
this body is honey
this body's got the juice
this body is like Prince Paul's production
                on De La's *Buhlōōne Mindstate*
this body is performance art
this body is conceptual
this body is the break
this body is a work song
this body is a freight train
this body is a crossroads
this body is a playlist for radical self-love
this body is like AI playing MJ
this body is like Ben Wallace making his free throws

this body is like Ray Allen making that
             step-back three with 5.2 seconds left on the clock
             to win game 6 of the 2013 NBA finals
             then win game 7 to take the championship
this body is like Kawhi Leonard
             signing with the Tkaronto Raptors for a year
             breezing on in winning a championship
             making "Canadian" history
             then bouncing back to his home ground
             to play for the people and the place he comes from
this body is
this body is
this body is
this body razes cities
this body started a war
this body ended a war
this body is at 1,000 horsepower
this body is at 1,000 "whore's power"
this body is a rocky road
this body is a trick of the eye
this body shines
this body waters
this body is dream
this body is reality
this body is part settler
this body settles
this body is unsettled
this body is home
this body is a miracle and it's mine
this body came from my yt mama
and I love it, and I love her

acknowledgments

For some time now I have questioned the use of Territorial acknowledgments, as institutions that uphold yt supremacist structures have begun to deploy them in attempts to be perceived as conciliatory in this era of "Reconciliation." As a non-Indigenous person, I have directly benefitted from the theft of this land now known as Canada.

This book is indebted to Lindsay Nixon's *nîtisânak*, their phenomenal memoir about queer Indigenous life on the prairies. Years ago I wrote a poem about my mother that I kept returning to, finally seeing what I could grow it into after reading *nîtisânak*. Also, though I'd seen "yt" used as social-media shorthand, Nixon's book is the first I'd read that changed the orthography of the word, destabilizing the concept of ytness by frequently naming it, and then changing the spelling of that naming to non-standard English, so I wanted to do that too. Lastly, Nixon's book reminded me to remember my youth and my queer kin in the prairies, and of what I miss about where I come from: kisiskāciwani-sīpiy (the South Saskatchewan River), the big sky in all of its permutations of blue, the wild roses.

In 2019 I was able to attend Growing Room, *Room* magazine's annual literary festival. It commenced with a full day of Indigenous Brilliance, an Indigenous reading series organized by Jessica Johns, jaye simpson, Emily Dundas Oke, and Patricia Massy of Massy Books, Vancouver's first Indigenous bookstore. I was so excited I couldn't sleep the night before. The programming was FIRE. Salia Joseph opened the day by welcoming us to the Territory, reminded those of us who are not from here that "if you're here, you better be making something beautiful." I got to hear Brandi Bird, Lindsay Nixon, Eden Robinson, Valeen Jules, Katherena Vermette, Arielle Twist, and Alicia Elliott (who I heard on a different day of the festival). My bag was heavy with books to get signed. I fangirled so hard, was awkward and disorganized in my speech, a sweaty, stinky, jangly mess of excitement, caffeine, and anxiety. Jessica and jaye were incredible MCs, with Jessica in gorgeous Kihew and Rose earrings and jaye serving different killer looks throughout the day's events. The seed of this book was watered by the work and presence of these brilliant beings.

Amber Dawn's *Sub Rosa* is a dream I rested and recovered in while writing this book. I wish I had her novel while I was exiting the sex trade, and I am thankful for it now.

The poems "sue and jane write a story together" were written in collaboration with Michelle Kennedy.

sunlight, moonlight, starlight – Audra McDonald, Cecily Nicholson, Echo Kuo, Emily Fedoruk, Michelle Kennedy – I love you

citations

This book frequently cites settler vocabulary from two sources: F.W. Gershaw's historical account of Medicine Hat, *Saamis: The Medicine Hat* and Wikipedia, specifically the entries on Medicine Hat and Jerry Potts (last accessed September 2019). This vocabulary, italicized throughout, has been reiterated countless times in settler colonial writing. Parts of the Wikipedia entry on Potts are from the University of Toronto / Université Laval's online *Dictionary of Canadian Biography* entry on Potts.

"what we are / what they see"

"what we are/what they see" uses the term "pheneticize" from Wayde Compton's essay "Pheneticizing Versus Passing," in which he complicates the term "passing" and creates a new terminology for the ways in which people read race. Passing is "deliberately misrepresenting oneself racially" while pheneticizing is "racially perceiving someone based on subjective examination of his or her outward appearance." Someone like me is what Compton calls "phenopolysemic": "A person whose appearance can suggest more than one racial designation."

"this body"

The phrase "bbq pork-scented sorrow" is from Kai Cheng Thom's poem "diaspora babies" in *a place called No Homeland*. Check it out, as well as *Fierce Femmes and Notorious Liars: A Dangerous Trans Girl's Confabulous Memoir*, one of the best books I've ever read about sex work.

The phrase "whore's power" is from throat singer and writer Tanya Tagaq's tweet in which she says "every time I hear horsepower I think whore's power." Check out her albums and novel *Split Tooth*.

The lines about sovereignty were inspired by Fred Moten and Stefano Harney's "Improvement and Preservation: or, Usufruct and Use," Billy-Ray Belcourt's *This Wound Is a World* (Frontenac, 2017; University of Minnesota Press, 2019), and Sarah Hunt's question to Belcourt about sovereignty at UBC in 2017.

The line "could this body be medicine?" is inspired by Justin Ducharme's poem "dream boy" in *Hustling Verse: An Anthology of Sexworkers' Poetry*, edited by Amber Dawn and Justin (Arsenal Pulp Press, 2019). Check out Justin's poetry and films; his *Positions* is fire and was the first film I'd seen where I felt seen as a sexworker.

In March 2019 artists T'uy't'tanat-Cease Wyss and Anne Riley facilitated a workshop on making "seed bombs," wildflower seeds encased in spheres of mud from the Capilano River banks and compost from the Harmony Garden on Capilano Reserve that we participants made and then were to disperse as we saw fit; they also taught about the plant life around the Native Education College where the workshop took place.

The phrase "star seeded" is artist Sharona Franklin's IG handle. Check out Sharona's projects on disability and industrial healing at galleries across the continent and online @star_seeded and @paidtechnologies.

Mercedes Eng is a prairie-born poet of Chinese and settler descent living in Vancouver on the unceded Territories of the xʷməθkʷəy̓əm (Musqueam), Sḵwx̱wú7mesh (Squamish), and səl̓ilwətaʔɬ (Tsleil-Waututh) Nations. Eng's creative practice combines teaching in classrooms and on the ground, experiential knowledge, community organizing, independent study, and a hybrid poetics that deploys multiple forms of language from theory to memoir to historical and official state documents to art and photography. She is the author of *Mercenary English*, a long poem about sex work, violence, and resistance in the Downtown Eastside neighbourhood of Vancouver, and *Prison Industrial Complex Explodes*, winner of the 2018 Dorothy Livesay Poetry Prize. Her writing has appeared in *Hustling Verse: An Anthology of Sex Workers' Poetry*, *Jacket 2*, *Asian American Literary Review*, *The Capilano Review*, *The Abolitionist*, and *r/ally* (No One Is Illegal), *Survaillance*, and *M'aidez* (Press Release).